The Best Gift for Mom

by Lee Klein

Illustrated by Pam Keating

Paulist Press

New York / Mahwah, N.J.

Book and cover design by Saija Autrand, Faces Type & Design.

Library of Congress Cataloging-in-Publication Data

Klein, Lee, 1957–
    The best gift for Mom / by Lee Klein ; illustrated by Pam Keating.
        p.   cm.
    Summary: After learning more about his father, who had died
when he was a baby, Jonathan decides that he will sing a special song
for his mother in the school Christmas pageant.
    ISBN 0-8091-6627-5
    [1. Single-parent family—Fiction.   2. Mothers and sons—Fiction.
3. Death—Fiction.]   I. Keating, Pamela T., ill.   II. Title.
PZ7.K678335Be   1995
[Fic]—dc20   95-8665
                                                                 CIP
                                                                  AC

Published by Paulist Press
997 Macarthur Boulevard
Mahwah, New Jersey 07430

Printed and bound in the
United States of America

To my brother, Frank Young,
for raising me with a sense of compassion and
a sense of humor

and

To my three best friends: Gerry, Ellie and Jake.

Special thanks to:
Mrs. Greenberg's 1994–95 fourth grade class
at Frank G. Lindsey Elementary School
in Montrose, NY,
and
my editor, Karen Scialabba,
for understanding children and
understanding writers.

Today is December 26. Usually that's one of the worst days of the year for me because Christmas is over and I have to wait a whole year before it comes around again. But this year is different. I'm still excited because yesterday was the best Christmas my Mom and I ever had together.

The whole story started back in September . . .

It was the first day of school. My new teacher, Ms. Andrews, was getting acquainted with the class. We moved our chairs into a big circle.

"We'll take turns telling our names, and something about ourselves," she said. "Do you have any brothers or sisters? What does your mother do? What does your father do?"

The last question made me uncomfortable. I thought about saying, "None of your business," but that's really not fair. After all, how was Ms. Andrews supposed to know that my father died when I was a baby? I don't remember him at all, but we have pictures and my Mom tells me stories about him.

Sean, who sat next to me, told the class his father was a policeman. Then it was my turn. "Here goes," I thought, taking a deep breath.

"My name is Jonathan. I'm an only child, and I like it. My mother's name is Danielle and she's a graphic artist. She works for a big company."

Ms. Andrews waited for a moment instead of going on to the next person. A girl sitting across from me named Elena asked, "What about your father? What does your father do?"

"I don't have a father," I explained. "He died."

The whole class got very quiet. I saw the sad look on Ms. Andrews' face.

"It's O.K., Ms. Andrews, really," I told her. "It was a long time ago." That's what was hard about not having a father—the sorry looks on people's faces when they first found out.

"Thank you, Jonathan," Ms. Andrews finally said.

That afternoon on the playground, Sean asked me, "Hey, Jonathan. Did your Dad really die?"

"Yeah."

"How did he die? Was he killed or something?" another boy I hardly knew asked.

That was a tough question to answer. I'm not exactly sure. My mom said it was from cancer, but I don't know much about cancer. So I decided to give an easier answer.

"Yeah, he was killed in the war."

"Wow!" said Sean. "How?"

"Well, he was fighting in the army. It was during the war in Vietnam."

"Who killed him?"

"We don't know. Everybody shoots at everybody during a battle," I said. I was starting to feel that my lie was going to grow into a bigger one, so I changed the subject fast.

"Come on," I said grabbing Sean's arm. "Let's go play kickball!"

After school, I went to daycare at Mrs. Arnold's house. I like Mrs. Arnold. She has snacks that taste good, even though they're healthy. She also has a big basement in her house with a lot of matchbox cars and a track, building sets, and, best of all, a computer with games on it.

I decided to play by myself that afternoon, instead of with Elena who goes to Mrs. Arnold's too. I guess I played for a long time, trying to beat the computer at checkers, but it seemed like only a few minutes. Then I heard my Mom coming to pick me up.

"I'm finally here," she said to Mrs. Arnold.
"I'm so sorry I'm late! I didn't mean to keep you."
I heard her footsteps rushing down the stairs.
"Oh, and I'm the last parent here. I'm sorry, honey,"
she said, leaning over to give me a kiss on the head.
I hate kisses, especially in front of people, even
Mrs. Arnold. I had to hold out my arm to block her.

"Mom, I didn't even notice you were late. Can we stay a few more minutes so I can finish this game?"

"Stay? No, no, I'm sorry, Jonathan. We don't have time. We have to have dinner, then your bath, and it's late already. Hurry up! Get your book bag. Let's go! Aren't you hungry?" she asked, rushing me out the door.

I wasn't, but I remembered that my mom probably was.

"Sure," I said. "Can we have pizza?"

"Are you sure you're not mad at me for being late?" she asked me when we got in the car. She had that "concerned mother" voice.

"I'm sure," I said. Mom worries a lot about those things.

"It was an unexpected emergency. I'm designing a new cereal box! You can't believe what a hurry those cereal people are in! They want the work done right away! I wish I didn't have to work so much, honey," she sighed.

"You don't have to work that much. Most of my friends' mothers work too," I reminded her. "My new friend Sean's mom even has to work at night. She's a nurse."

Mom's face relaxed. She even smiled. "So, tell me all about third grade," she said.

Later that night at bedtime, Mom came into my room to say goodnight. Before she turned out the light, I decided to ask her about something that was bothering me.

"Mom, Dad didn't die in the army, did he?"

"No, your father was already out of the army before I met him. Don't you remember that I explained to you how he died?"

"Yeah, I guess I just got mixed up. But did he carry a gun and grenades and stuff?"

Mom smiled. "There are a lot of different jobs that need to be done in the army. Some soldiers leave the country and some take care of things right here."

"Where was Dad?"

"Fort Dix, New Jersey."

"Can we go there sometime and visit?"

"Sure."

"What did Dad do after he left the army?"

"He went on to college and had to pass some very hard tests. When he graduated, he was an accountant. He was very good at math!"

"What else did he do?"

"Oh, let me try to remember. He liked to tell silly jokes, he liked playing tennis, and he liked going camping."

"Mom, do you think Dad would be mad if I told a lie about him?"

"What lie?" she asked.

I told her about the conversation earlier that day on the playground. Mom thought for a while, staring at the ceiling. Then she answered, "I think Dad would understand why you told a lie. But *I* want you to know the truth and be able to say it the next time anyone asks you. Got it?"

"Got it."

"O.K. It's late. Get to sleep!"

After Mom turned out the light and went to bed, I stayed awake for a while thinking about a story she had told me a long time ago about my father.

When I was about a year old, my parents would
take turns putting me to bed at night. Mom would
rock me in the rocking chair and make up stories
about bunnies and puppies. She would talk softly
until I fell asleep in her arms; then she would
carefully lay me down in my crib.

Dad had a different way. He would put me in
the crib and gently rub my back while singing.

Dad didn't really know the words to any quiet songs, so he sang the only one he could remember. It was called "Taps" and it's the song the bugler used to play every night when he was in the army.

Then, on my first Christmas eve, the three of us went to church. The choir sang a lot of pretty Christmas carols. Dad was holding me in his arms when the choir sang "Silent Night" and found himself softly singing along. By the end of the song, I had fallen asleep.

"Well," Mom whispered to him, "I'm happy to hear you know another song!"

For the next couple of months, Dad sang "Silent Night" when it was his turn to put me to bed.

Before that winter was over, my father began having pains in his back. He went to the doctor. Then that doctor sent him to another special doctor who knows a lot about cancer and how to treat it. But his cancer was a very bad kind that got worse quickly, so the doctor couldn't make him better.

When Dad died, my mother missed him very much. But she was thankful that she and I still had each other. I am too.

Sometimes I think about what it would be like if
Dad was with us. My family would be more like my
friends' families. Dad might take me on weekends
to the ballfield to practice my pitching, instead of
Mom. I would tell everyone at school about him
and he'd tell everyone at work about me.

I wonder if that's why God gave me a Mom who can really catch, and who keeps pictures of me on her desk at work.

The next morning at school, we went to music class. The music teacher is Mr. Cooley, but he lets us call him "Mr. Cool."

"All right, everybody, settle down," Mr. Cool said. "We're going to warm up our voices, then learn some music for our first concert, which will be around Christmas time."

Sean and I fooled around a little bit when the class was supposed to be singing scales.

"Now I'm going to give some of you lines to sing all by yourselves," he announced. Some the students put their hands in the air and shouted, "Pick me, Mr. Cool! Please?" showing Mr. Cooley that they wanted to sing alone. But I sat on my hands and tried to look invisible. It didn't work.

"Here you go, Jonathan, the best line in the song."

The song was "The Twelve Days of Christmas." My line was "Five Golden Rings."

Mr. Cooley began playing the piano, nodding at each person when it was time for them to sing.

I felt as if I had butterflies in my stomach. Then Mr. Cooley nodded to me and said, "Give it all you've got, Jonathan." Before I could stop and think about it, I did exactly what the music teacher told me to do.

"FIVE GOLDEN RINGS" I sang out loud. Some of my friends looked surprised, but some said, "That was great!" Mr. Cooley said, "Now, let's have everyone sing as loudly and clearly as Jonathan."

Every time they came to my line, I sang it out even louder. At the end of the class, my friends clapped and I even took a bow.

A few weeks after that, it was October and time for soccer tryouts. A lot of my friends were trying out, but I had other interests this year.

"What do you mean you don't want to play?" Mom said. I couldn't tell if she was angry or just surprised. "You loved playing soccer last year."

"I didn't love it, I liked it," I reminded her. Then I told her the news. "You know what I really want to do?"

"What?" she asked.

"I want to join the glee club. I might want to be
a singer when I grow up."

"Where did all this interest come from?"

"Well, Mr. Cooley, my music teacher, says I'm a
really good singer and he might give one of the big
parts in the concert to me."

"But what about sports? I think you should be involved with sports, Jonathan. It's important to get exercise! It's important to be part of a team!"

"I will, Mom. I'll still play basketball in the winter and baseball in the spring." I love baseball.

"Jonathan, do you think if I could be home more and coach your soccer team you would like it better?" she asked.

"No!" I insisted. She was worrying again.

"O.K., we'll give it a try," she finally said. Then she leaned over to give me another one of those kisses.

I managed to shield myself from the kiss, but I felt like giving her a big hug!

The next two months, I went to glee club rehearsals after school before going to daycare. Mr. Cooley even gave me a whole song to sing by myself at the concert.

Everything was fine, until December. Then I noticed Mom seemed to become more quiet and sad as the days got closer and closer to Christmas time. I remembered that she was this way on Thanksgiving, too.

"Mom, how come you're so quiet?" I finally asked her one night after dinner.

"Me? I guess I was just thinking."

"About what?"

"Well, I was wishing that I could give you more, Jonathan."

"More? Like more video games?" I asked hopefully.

"No, you have plenty of those! I wish there were more than twenty-four hours in a day! Then we'd have time before dinner to skate on the frozen pond, or bake your favorite peanut butter chocolate chip cookies. We only have time for those things on the weekends, and even then we usually spend most of the time running errands."

"Stop worrying so much, Mom," I reminded her. "It's a waste of *time*."

"That's right, it is. You're getting pretty smart in your old age."

"Besides, I have a surprise for you for Christmas and you'll never guess what it is." It was hard for me to keep it a secret, but I was thinking about how happy she was going to be to hear me sing my solo in the Christmas concert.

Finally, the day of the concert arrived. Ms. Andrews complained that our class had been behaving on the wild side the past few weeks. We were excited about the holidays we would celebrate at the end of the month.

"Are you nervous about tonight, Jonathan?" Elena asked me.

"A little, I guess," I said, but on the inside
I could feel myself smiling.

"Your attention, class!" Ms. Andrews announced.
"Even though there is a performance tonight, you
still have homework! Remember to write a full page
letter to your pen pal and be ready to hand it in
tomorrow."

"Oh no, homework!" we all groaned.

Backstage that night, I tried to peek out at the audience through the curtain. I was wearing my new white shirt and tie. Before I could find my mother in the audience, the curtain began to open, and Mr. Cooley was playing the opening number.

"The Twelve Days of Christmas" was a hit and
everyone laughed at "five golden rings." "Jingle
Bells" was so lively that the audience clapped along
as we sang. Finally, it was time for my solo. I stepped

to the front of the stage the way Mr. Cooley had told me to, and then slowly began the melody of "Silent Night."

I was careful to pronounce each word clearly. There was no laughing or clapping along; the audience just listened. Finally, I held the last note as long as I could, until Mr. Cooley played the last chord. The parents clapped very loudly now. When I took a bow, I was thinking about how good I felt, but I was also hoping my Mom liked her surprise.

I found her in the school lobby after the concert. She was smiling, but her eyes were red and I could see that tears were drying on her cheeks.

"Mom! Are you O.K.?"

"Stop worrying so much, Jonathan," she joked. "I'm just crying because I'm so happy. That was the best Christmas present I ever had."

"Better than peanut butter chocolate chip cookies?" I asked.

"Better than anything. I love you, Jonathan," she said. Then she leaned forward to kiss me on the head, and this time I let her.

That night, while Mom read a book, I got out
my homework. But instead of writing to my pen pal,
whom I hardly knew, I decided I might as well write
a letter to someone else I hardly knew instead —
my father. Even though he couldn't read it, I wanted
to write my thoughts down:

Dear Dad,

I'm not sure if you can see me or not, so in case you can't, I thought I'd tell you about myself. I know you know my name, and my mother of course, but I've grown a lot since you've seen me.

I'm in third grade. I'm pretty smart, but sometimes I have trouble in reading. I have a best friend, Sean, and a lot of other friends. I love baseball and glee club. Tonight I was a big hit in the school concert. I think you would have been proud of me. I'm proud of you too. Mom says you were a great Dad and a great accountant. I wish I had known you longer.

Mom's doing a terrific job, too, but I don't think she always knows it. Is there any way you can let her know? I'll keep telling her also.

I have to go to bed now, but I'll write again soon.

Love,
Jonathan

P.S. Is it O.K. with you if I become a singer?
P.P.S. Tomorrow Mom's going to teach me "Taps."